D0742862

SLIM GOODBODY'S NUTRITION EDITION

Glorious Grains

Crabtree Publishing Company

www.crabtreebooks.com

Series development, writing, and packaging:
John Burstein, Slim Goodbody Corp.

Editors:
Molly Aloian
Reagan Miller
Mark Sachner, Water Buffalo Books

Editorial director:
Kathy Middleton

Production coordinator:
Kenneth Wright

Prepress technician:
Kenneth Wright

Designer:
Tammy West, Westgraphix LLC

Photos:
Chris Pinchback, Pinchback Photography

Photo credits:
© Slim Goodbody, iStockphotos, and Shutterstock images.

"Slim Goodbody" and Pinchback photos, copyright,
© Slim Goodbody

Acknowledgements:
The author would like to thank the following people for their help in this project:
Christine Burstein, Olivia Davis, Kylie Fong, Nathan Levig, Havana Lyman, Andrew McBride, Lulu McClure, Ben McGinnis, Esme Power, Joe Ryan

"Slim Goodbody" and "Slim Goodbody's Nutrition Edition" are registered trademarks of the Slim Goodbody Corp.

Library and Archives Canada Cataloguing in Publication

Burstein, John
        Glorious grains / John Burstein.

(Slim Goodbody's nutrition edition)
Includes index.
ISBN 978-0-7787-5043-7 (bound).--ISBN 978-0-7787-5058-1 (pbk.)

        1. Grain in human nutrition--Juvenile literature. 2. Nutrition--Juvenile literature. I. Title. II. Series:°Burstein, John. Slim Goodbody's nutrition edition.

QP144.G73B87 2010   j641.3'31   C2009-903855-2

Library of Congress Cataloging-in-Publication Data

Burstein, John.
        Glorious grains / John Burstein.
            p. cm. -- (Slim Goodbody's nutrition edition)
        Includes index.
        ISBN 978-0-7787-5043-7 (reinforced lib. bdg. : alk. paper) -- ISBN 978-0-7787-5058-1 (pbk. : alk. paper)
        1. Grain in human nutrition--Juvenile literature. 2. Nutrition--Juvenile literature. 3. Children--Nutrition--Requirements--Juvenile literature. I. Title. II. Series.

QP144.G73B87 2010
613.2--dc22

                                                        2009024578

Crabtree Publishing Company

www.crabtreebooks.com   1-800-387-7650

CONTENTS

GREETINGS

My name is Slim Goodbody.
I want to ask you two questions.

1. Do you like to eat good foods?
   I hope you said **YES**.

2. What can help show you what
   foods to eat?
   I hope you said

   THE FOOD PYRAMID.

The food pyramid helps you eat right.

There are six stripes on the U.S. food pyramid.

The stripes stand for the five different food groups plus oils.

GRAINS
VEGETABLES
FRUITS
OILS
MILK
MEAT
& BEANS

This book is about the grains food group.

GRAINS!

Grains belong on the orange stripe in the U.S. food pyramid.

Toast is a food made with grain.

Cereal is a food made with grain.

Every day you need to eat food made with grain.

Spaghetti is a food made with grain.

Pizza is a food made with grain.

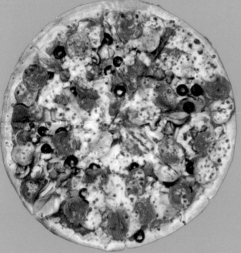

Tacos are a food made with grain.

GRAINS COME FROM PLANTS

Different grains come from different plants.

corn

rice

wheat

Different grain plants look different.

sorghum

barley

millet

oats

rye

WHOLE GRAIN FOODS

The grains we eat are the seeds of grain plants. A grain seed has three parts. The three parts are the germ, the bran, and the endosperm.

SEED

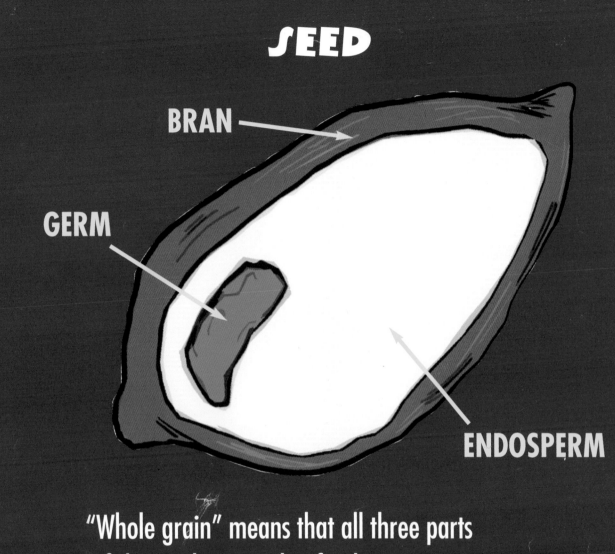

BRAN

GERM

ENDOSPERM

"Whole grain" means that all three parts
of the seed are used in food.

FIELD TO TABLE

How can a seed
Planted down in a hole
Wind up as cereal
Poured in your bowl?

Here is a list
Of the steps that it takes
To turn corn in a field
Into corn in cornflakes.

Grains start out on farms.

STEP 1

When the corn is high, the farmer cuts it down.

STEP 2

The corn goes to a mill. The corn kernels are taken off the cob. They are cooked, dried, and flattened into cornflakes.

STEP 3

The cornflakes are put into cereal boxes and driven to the store.

STEP 4

Your parents bring the cereal home. At breakfast, you pour the cornflakes into your bowl.

AROUND THE WORLD

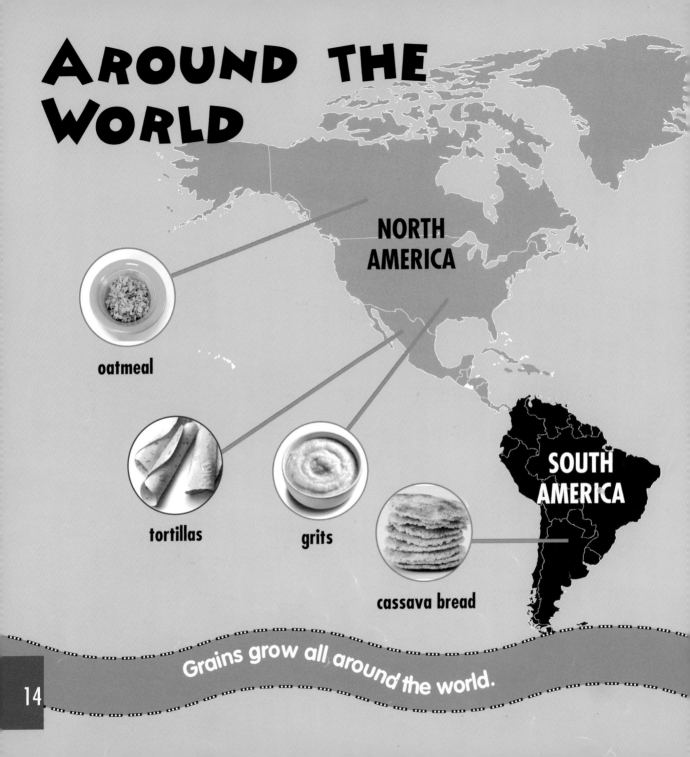

NORTH AMERICA

oatmeal

tortillas

grits

cassava bread

SOUTH AMERICA

Grains grow all around the world.

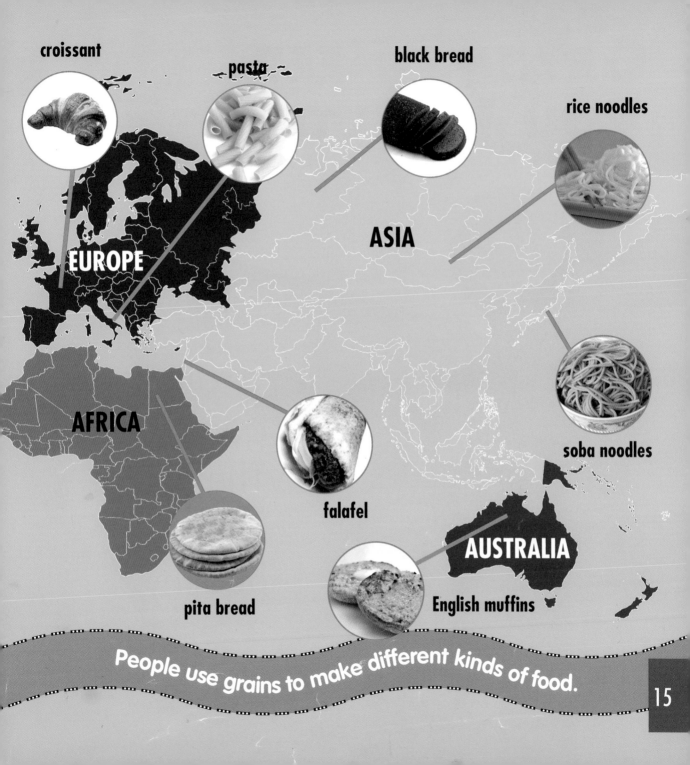

croissant

pasta

black bread

rice noodles

EUROPE

ASIA

AFRICA

soba noodles

falafel

AUSTRALIA

pita bread

English muffins

People use grains to make different kinds of food.

15

GRAINS KEEP YOU HEALTHY

Grains are good for you. They help keep you healthy.

Grains help different body parts.

Grains help your heart work well.

Grains help you digest your food.

Grains give your muscles energy to move.

Grains are good for your brain and nerves.

Grains help your body make blood cells.

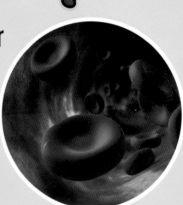

Grains help your bones grow strong.

WHAT COUNTS AS AN OUNCE?

You need to eat four to five ounces (113 to 142 grams) of grains every day.

Try to eat different kinds of grains, such as barley, oats, and rye.

HERE IS WHAT COUNTS AS AN OUNCE:

1 slice whole wheat toast
½ an English muffin
1 "mini" bagel
1 pancake
1 small tortilla
1 cup of cooked pasta
1 small biscuit
1 small piece of
   corn bread
1 small muffin

5 whole wheat crackers
½ cup of cooked cereal
   (such as oatmeal)
1 cup of whole-grain
   cold breakfast cereal
½ cup of cooked brown rice
1 hamburger bun
3 cups of low-fat popcorn

1 cup = 250 ml   1/2 cup = 125 ml

19

Almost any time is a good time to eat grains.

You can have a bowl of whole-grain cereal in the morning.

You can have a tasty pita sandwich at lunch.

You can snack on some crackers after school.

You can have some whole-wheat spaghetti for dinner.

You can eat low-fat popcorn for a tasty treat!

WORLD FOOD GUIDES

The U.S. food pyramid is only one guide to eating well.

To learn more about Canada's Food Guide, check out the Web site below.

http://www.nms.on.ca/Elementary/canada.htm

People from different parts of the world often eat different kinds of foods. People use different food guides to help them eat wisely.

GREAT INDIAN FOOD PYRAMID

Butter
oil ..>
fruits ..>
pulses ..>
veg ..>
milk ..>
cereals ..>
AT

Every day, everyone, everywhere needs grains.

WORDS TO KNOW

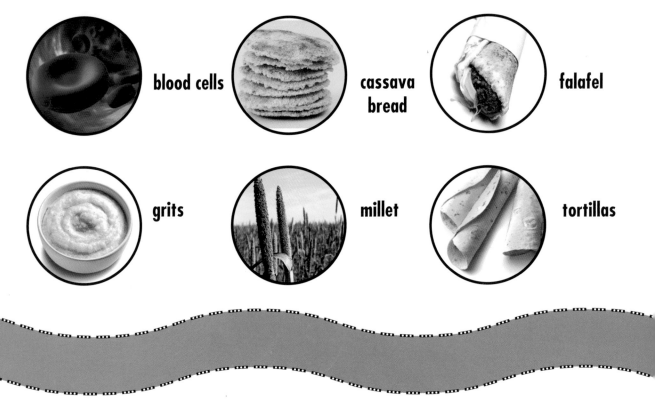

blood cells

cassava bread

falafel

grits

millet

tortillas

FIND OUT MORE

Books

Grains To Bread, Inez Snyder, Children's Press.

Grains and Cereals, Sally Hewitt, Hodder Wayland.

Web Sites

MyPyramid.gov
www.mypyramid.gov/kids/index.html

Slim Goodbody
www.slimgoodbody.com

Printed in the U.S.A.-CG